GENERATION CRICKET

GLOBAL CRICKET

Clive Gifford

First published in 2015 by Wayland
Copyright © Wayland 2015

Wayland
338 Euston Road
London NW1 3BH

Wayland Australia
Level 17/207 Kent Street
Sydney, NSW 2000

Editor: Elizabeth Brent
Designer: Peter Clayman

Dewey number: 796.3'58-dc23

ISBN 978 0 7502 9270 2
eBook ISBN 978 0 7502 9271 9

Printed in China

10 9 8 7 6 5 4 3 2 1

2

Picture acknowledgements: Cover: © Charlie Crowhurst/Getty images (main), © Scott Heavey/Getty images (bl), © Mitchell Gunn/Getty images (bm), © Charlie Crowhurst/Getty images; p1: © Getty images/Manoj Patil/Hindustan Times; p2: © Scott Barbour/Getty images; p4: © Morne de Klerk/Getty images; p5: © Matthew Lewis-iDi/iDi/ Getty images (t), © Stu Forster/Getty images (b); p6: © Getty images (t), © DESHAKALYAN CHOWDHURY/AFP/Getty images (b); p7: © Robert Prezioso/Getty images (t), © Matthew Lewis/Getty images (m), © MUNIR UZ ZAMAN/AFP/Getty images (b); p8: © Michael Dodge/Getty images (l), © Randy Brooks/Getty images Latin America for CPL (r); p9: © Gareth Copley/Getty images (r); p10: © SESHADRI SUKUMAR/AFP/Gettyimages; p11: © Mitchell Gunn/Getty images (r), Sattish Bate/ Hindustan Times via Getty images (l); p12: © EMMANUEL DUNAND/AFP/Getty images; p13: © Scott Barbour/Getty images (tl), © JEKESAI NJIKIZANA/AFP/Getty images (tr), © Matthew Lewis-iDi/iDi via Getty images (b); p14: © Stu Forster/Getty images; p15 © Nigel Roddis/Getty images (l), © Simon Watts/Getty images (r); p16: AAMIR QURESHI/AFP/Gettyimages; p17: © Harry Engels-iCC/iCC via Getty images (br), Gareth Copley/Getty images (l), PAUL ELLIS/AFP/Getty images (tr); p18: © Graham Crouch/Getty images (l), © STAN HONDA/AFP/Getty images (r); p19: © Daniel Berehulak/ Getty images (tl), © Daniel Berehulak-iPL 2010/iPL via Getty images (tr), © Hamish Blair/Getty images (br); p20: © Graham Crouch/iCC via Getty images; p21: © INDRANIL MUKHERJEE/AFP/Getty images (tl), © Pal Pillai-iDi/iDi via Getty images (bl), © Pal Pillai-iDi/iDi via Getty images (tr); p22 © Charlie Crowhurst/Getty images; p23: © David Munden/Popperfoto/Getty images (t), © Robert Prezioso/Getty images (m), © Tertius Pickard/Gallo images/Getty images; p24: © PAUL ELLIS/AFP/Getty images; p25: © Fox Photos/Hulton Archive/Getty images (t), © IAN KINGTON/AFP/Getty images (bl), © Ben Hoskins/Getty images (br); p26: © Harry Engels/Getty images; p27 © Stefan Gosatti/Getty images (t), © GLYN KIRK/AFP/Getty images (b); p28: © Gareth Copley/Getty images; p29: © Scott Barbour/Getty images (l), © Michael Dodge/Getty images (t), © GREG WOOD/AFP/Getty images (b). All graphic elements are courtesy of Shutterstock.com.

The website addresses (URLs) included in this book were valid at the time of going to press. However, it is possible that contents or addresses may have changed since the publication of this book. No responsibility for any such changes can be accepted by either the author or the Publisher.

Wayland is a division of Hachette Children's Books, an Hachette UK company.
www.hachette.co.uk

Contents

The world of cricket 4

Cricket for all 6

Twenty20 8

The IPL 10

ICC World Twenty20 12

Limited overs cricket 14

One Day Internationals 16

The ICC World Cup 18

The ICC Women's Cricket World Cup 20

First class cricket 22

Test match cricket 24

Test nations 26

The Ashes 28

Glossary 30

Further information 31

Index 32

3

The world of cricket

If you want action, drama and tension, then cricket is the game for you! With fielders diving at full stretch, shots flying out of the ground and balls being bowled at more than 140km/h, all in front of colourful, noisy crowds, cricket can be great entertainment.

Players and teams

Cricket offers an exciting test of players' fitness, athleticism, reactions and skills as two teams try to outplay each other. Sometimes, a complete team performance such as sharp bowling and fielding by all eleven cricketers wins one team the game. On other occasions, magnificent individual performances by a batsman or a bowler lead to victory.

Cricket has even reached the South Pole. In 2012 a British team of adventurers played a game of cricket against a Rest of the World team made up of scientists from an Antarctic research station. In temperatures of –35°C, the British team won!

Fans at the Adelaide Oval watch the second Test between Australia and England.

BIGGEST CROWDS AT A TEST MATCH DAY

100,000	India v Pakistan	Kolkata, 1999
91,112	Australia v England	Melbourne, 2013
90,800	Australia v West Indies	Melbourne, 1961
89,155	Australia v England	Melbourne, 2006

A big-hitting batsman, Afridi was only 16 years old when he scored his first hundred in a One Day International (ODI) for Pakistan. He has since scored over 7,600 runs in ODIs, many struck with great force, hence his nickname Boom Boom. In a 2013 ODI against South Africa, Afridi hit the ball out of the ground, a shot measured at an incredible 158m.

SHAHID AFRIDI

All around the world

World cricket is run by the International Cricket Council (ICC). The ICC has a whopping 106 member nations from Afghanistan to Zimbabwe, all of whom play cricket both in their home countries and abroad in international matches. The top ten nations play Test cricket, the longest form of the game, with matches lasting five days. At the other end of the scale are lightning-fast Twenty20 (T20) games, which are over in two or three hours.

Ian Bell dives to try and stop a shot from Indian batsman Abhinav Mukund during a 2011 Test match in England.

5

Cricket for all

You may think of cricket as a game played on large grassy grounds by men in white clothing, but the sport is far more varied than that. Everyone can play a version of the game, no matter where or who they are. Cricket is played by men and women, boys and girls in all sorts of locations from casual games in streets, parks and back gardens to beaches all over the world.

Indoor cricket

Cricket is even played indoors, in large sports halls. Indoor cricket still has two batsmen who score runs both by running, as in normal cricket, and also by hitting the ball into certain areas of the nets which are hung around the pitch. There's even an Indoor Cricket World Cup which Australia have won eight times, their last victory being in 2011 when they beat South Africa in the final.

An indoor cricket match, with fielders positioned to try to catch the ball and nets surrounding the pitch.

Boys play a casual game of cricket on a beach in Sri Lanka's capital city of Colombo. Beach cricket is played all over the world.

In 2000, Saijida Shah played her first international game for Pakistan against the Ireland women's team. She was just 12 years old! Three years later, in a game against the Japanese national team, she took seven wickets for just four runs.

A brilliant wicketkeeper and an aggressive batter, Taylor was just 19 when she became the youngest woman to reach 1,000 runs scored in One Day Internationals (ODIs). She has now scored almost 3,000 ODI runs, including five centuries, and was voted T20 International Women's Cricketer of the Year in 2013. In the same year, she played for Walmley's men's cricket team.

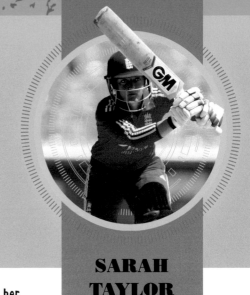

SARAH TAYLOR

A young girl misses the ball with her shot in a Kwik Cricket game with England women's captain Charlotte Edwards looking on.

Kwik Cricket

Known as Walla Cricket in Australia, Kwik Cricket is a scaled-down version of the sport, designed to get younger children into the game. Stumps, ball and bat are made of plastic and teams are often eight a side. Everyone gets a go at bowling, batting and fielding in different positions.

Women's cricket

Cricket has been played by women and girls for more than a century, whilst the first Women's Test match occurred between Australia and England in 1934. It's only in recent years, though, that the sport has boomed with thousands more female players taking part. More and more nations are sending women's teams to compete in international tournaments where stars such as Charlotte Edwards, Ellyse Perry and Stafanie Taylor are gaining major media attention.

Australia's Elyse Villani hits a shot during the World T20 Final in 2014 with Sarah Taylor poised behind the stumps. Australia went on to win the game and tournament.

Twenty20

Cricket changed in 2003 with the introduction of a new, shorter form of the game for top players. Twenty20 saw teams given just 20 overs to build a score. It was a style of game familiar to many amateur cricketers who play 20-overs-a-side matches in evenings and at weekends. T20 has caught on big time and now attracts large, boisterous crowds.

Bat v ball

T20 adjusts cricket's rules to favour quick, big hitting. No bowler can bowl more than four overs whilst for the first six overs, only two fielders can be placed outside a 30-yard circle drawn around the pitch. This encourages batsmen to "go over the top", hitting the ball for boundaries. Batsmen don't have it all their own way, though. T20 fielding is sharp, run-outs happen all the time and bowlers have learned to bowl cannily to dry up the flow of runs and heap pressure on the batters, who have to score quickly as soon as they come in to bat.

Lendl Simmons hits a six for Guyana Amazon Warriors during the final of the Caribbean Premier League in 2013.

Big-hitting Aaron Finch comes out to bat for the Melbourne Renegades during a 2014 Big Bash game against local rivals, Melbourne Stars.

Scott Styris has scored the most runs from a single T20 over – an incredible 38 runs due to two no balls for Sussex against Gloucestershire in 2012. He went on to make a century off of only 37 balls.

National competitions

All the major cricketing nations have their own T20 competition for regional sides, from New Zealand's HRV Cup to the Caribbean Premier League in the West Indies. In England, the T20 Blast began in 2014 and features 18 teams who play 14 games each with the top four sides entering semi-finals. In Australia, the Big Bash sees eight city-based teams battle to reach the final, won in 2014 by the Perth Scorchers.

The world record for best bowling figures in a T20 match is held by a player not from England, India or Australia but from Malaysia. Arul Suppiah grabbed six wickets for just five runs whilst playing for Somerset versus Glamorgan in 2011.

HIGHEST TOTALS IN T20 INTERNATIONALS

260	Sri Lanka v Kenya	2007
248	Australia v England	2013
241	South Africa v England	2009
225	Ireland v Afghanistan	2013
221	Australia v England	2007

T20 internationals

England and New Zealand's women played the first T20 between national teams back in 2004. T20 men's internationals began the following year. Australian Aaron Finch hit the highest T20 international score against England in 2013. His 156 runs came off just 63 balls and featured 11 fours and 14 sixes.

England celebrate taking a wicket in a 2014 T20 versus Sri Lanka.

The IPL

First held in 2008, the Indian Premier League (IPL) is one of the most glamourous and popular tournaments in world cricket. Every April, top players from around the world gather in India to play in this six-week-long festival of cricket. The stadiums are packed with fans for every match, and the players are treated like superstars, idolised wherever they go.

2014 TEAMS
- Chennai Super Kings
- Delhi Daredevils
- Sunrisers Hyderabad
- Kings XI Punjab
- Kolkata Knight Riders
- Mumbai Indians
- Rajasthan Royals
- Royal Challengers Bangalore

Format

The IPL is a Twenty20 competition. In 2014, eight teams contested the trophy. They played each other twice in a league, with the top four going through to knockout semi-finals and the final. The winners played an exhausting 15 matches over an intense six-week period of competition.

Kolkata Knight Riders celebrate winning the 2012 IPL after beating Chennai Super Kings in the final game.

DLF INDIAN PREMIER LEAGUE CHAMPIONS 2012

Gayle force

The best innings in the IPL was hit by West Indian opener Chris Gayle, who smashed 175 runs in just 66 balls playing for the Royal Challengers Bangalore against the Pune Warriors India on 23 April 2013. He hit a record 17 sixes and 13 fours, taking his team to the highest ever team score of 263 for 5. Gayle has hit 196 sixes – the most in the IPL.

Chris Gayle strikes a fierce shot during a quickfire innings of 57 off just 31 balls for the Royal Challengers Bangalore against the Pune Warriors India.

LASITH MALINGA

Sri Lankan fast bowler Lasith Malinga is the highest wicket-taker in the history of the IPL, with 100 wickets in 70 matches. He is an expert at bowling 'at the death', when batsmen are looking to hit boundaries every ball. With his unique round-arm action, 'Slinger' Malinga spears in 145-kph balls at the batsmen's feet, making it very hard to score.

PAST FINALISTS
2008: Chennai Super Kings vs Rajasthan Royals (winners)
2009: Deccan Chargers (winners) vs Royal Challengers Bangalore
2010: Mumbai Indians vs Chennai Super Kings (winners)
2011: Chennai Super Kings (winners) vs Royal Challengers Bangalore
2012: Chennai Super Kings vs Kolkata Knight Riders (winners)
2013: Chennai Super Kings vs Mumbai Indians (winners)
2014: Kings XI Punjab vs Kolkata Knight Riders (winners)

ICC World Twenty20

Not long after T20 games first grabbed the public's attention, the first world-cup-styled competition for national T20 teams was held in South Africa in 2007. The World Twenty20 promises, and often delivers, fast and furious action.

Kevin Pietersen strikes a six during England's victory over Australia in the 2010 World T20 final. Pietersen's 248 runs in the competition saw him awarded player of the tournament.

Big batting

The tournaments have seen some incredible batting, from Kevin Pietersen's 248 runs which helped England to win the 2010 competition to Yuvraj Singh's 50 off 20 balls in the semi-final of the 2007 tournament. Amazingly, this wasn't Yuvraj's fastest 50; earlier in the tournament he scored 50 off of just 12 balls!

HIGHEST INDIVIDUAL SCORES, 2014 WORLD T20

116 not out	Alex Hales	England
111 not out	Ahmed Shehzad	Pakistan
94	Umar Akmal	Pakistan
89	Mahela Jayawardene	Sri Lanka
86	Jean-Paul Duminy	South Africa

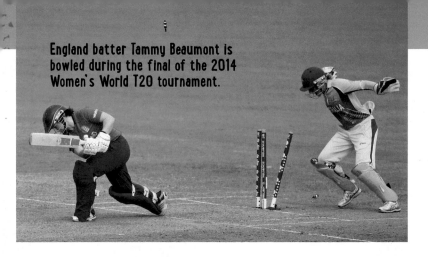

England batter Tammy Beaumont is bowled during the final of the 2014 Women's World T20 tournament.

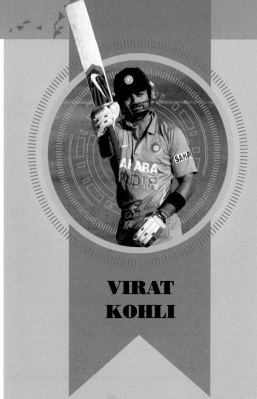

Women's World T20

First held in England, and won by England in 2009, the Women's World T20 sees eight or, as of 2014, 10 teams compete in two groups. The top teams then enter semi-finals and a final. Australia won the competition in 2010, 2012 and 2014, but two were very close. England lost by just four runs in the 2012 final and New Zealand by just three runs in 2010.

MS Dhoni leaps in celebration after catching Sri Lanka's Lahiru Thirimanne during the 2014 World T20 final.

VIRAT KOHLI

An excellent one-day player with over 5,600 ODI runs, including 19 centuries, Kohli has taken well to scoring quickly in T20, with 907 runs scored at a rapid pace. Kohli blasted a record 319 runs at the 2014 World T20, the most of any player at any World T20 tournament.

T20 WORLD CUP FINALISTS			
	Hosts	Winners	Runners-up
2007	South Africa	India	Pakistan
2009	England	Pakistan	Sri Lanka
2010	West Indies	England	Australia
2012	Sri Lanka	West Indies	Sri Lanka
2014	Bangladesh	Sri Lanka	India

Bowling and fielding

Whilst T20 games may seem to be all about runs, a brilliant bowling or fielding performance can turn a game around. Pakistan won the 2009 T20 World Cup largely due to Umar Gul's terrific bowling, which included taking five wickets for just six runs in their match against New Zealand. Sri Lanka's Ajantha Mendis went one better, taking six wickets for eight runs versus Zimbabwe at the 2012 tournament. A.B. de Villiers, playing as a fielder not a wicketkeeper, holds the record for the most catches – 21 in total.

Limited overs cricket

Long before there were T20 games, limited overs cricket provided a complete match in a day for teams and fans. The first professional limited overs games occurred in England in the 1960s and involved each team batting for 65 overs. Other competitions, all over the world, are now played to differing numbers of overs. Games in South Africa's South Bank Cup, for instance, are 45 overs per side.

Rikki Clarke runs out Brendan Nash during the 2014 Royal London Cup semi-final between Warwickshire Bears and Kent Spitfires. Warwickshire won the game but lost to Durham in the final.

ECB 40 RECORDS
Highest innings (batsman): 180 - Ryan ten Doeschate, Essex Eagles, 2013
Highest innings (team): 399 for 4 – Sussex Sharks v Worcestershire Royals, 2011
Lowest innings (team): 56 – the Netherlands v Worcestershire Royals, 2012
Best bowling figures: 7/29 - David Payne, Gloucestershire Gladiators, 2010
Most runs in a tournament: 861 - Jacques Rudolph, Yorkshire Carnegie, 2010

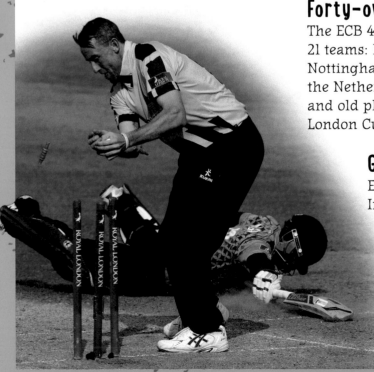

Forty-over fun

The ECB 40 was introduced in 2010 and featured 21 teams: 18 counties including 2013 winners, the Nottinghamshire Outlaws, plus the Scottish Saltires, the Netherlands and the Unicorns, a mixture of young and old players. In 2014, it was replaced by the Royal London Cup, a 50-over competition for the 18 counties.

Global limited overs

Eight teams contest the Super50, the West Indies' main limited overs tournament, whilst 20 take part in Sri Lanka's Premier Limited Overs tournament. The One Day Cup is Australia's main limited overs competition. With 11 championships, Western Australia have seen the most success, but the Queensland Bulls are just one championship behind after winning in both 2013 and 2014.

Durham all-rounder Ben Stokes bowls during a 2014 Royal London Cup game against Nottinghamshire Outlaws.

When Sussex Sharks scored 336 runs on their home ground in 2013, they must have thought they had their ECB 40 game won. But Kent Spitfires had other ideas and scored 337 with nine balls to spare!

Power plays

Power plays are a rule innovation in some limited over competitions. In power-play overs, only a small number of fielders are allowed outside of a 30-yard (27.4m) circle around the middle of the pitch. The aim is to create chances for batsmen to score boundaries but also to force fielding teams to be more attacking themselves, with more fielders close to the bat.

Tim McIntosh of the Auckland Aces bats against the Otago Volts as the Aces successfully chase 303 runs in New Zealand's Ford Trophy competition.

One Day Internationals

Blame the weather for inventing the One Day International (ODI). Rain had washed out a 1971 Test match between Australia and England when a limited overs game between the two teams was organised to entertain spectators. That match was 40 overs per side, other early ODIs were 55 or 60 overs per side, but today, ODIs are 50 overs per side.

Highs and lows

Many ODIs are high-scoring affairs. Teams often score five or six runs per over throughout their innings. The team batting second have to deal with the pressure of chasing their opponent's score. In a 2006 ODI, Australia scored the most ODI runs ever, finishing with a score of 434. Yet, amazingly, South Africa won, scoring 438 and winning with just one ball to spare. In contrast, the lowest-ever ODI total was 35, when Zimbabwe were bowled out by Sri Lanka in 2004.

SPEEDY CENTURY
The fastest ever ODI century was scored by New Zealand batsman Corey Anderson against the West Indies in 2014. Anderson's hundred came in only 36 balls, took just 35 minutes and featured 12 sixes.

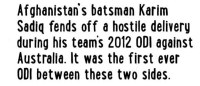

Afghanistan's batsman Karim Sadiq fends off a hostile delivery during his team's 2012 ODI against Australia. It was the first ever ODI between these two sides.

MOST ODI WICKETS

Wickets	Player	Best bowling
534	Muttiah Muralitharan	7 for 30
502	Wasim Akram	5 for 15
416	Waqar Younis	7 for 36
400	Chaminda Vaas	8 for 19
393	Shaun Pollock	6 for 35

Jos Buttler strikes the ball powerfully during England's ODI versus Sri Lanka at Lords. Buttler scored 121 runs off just 74 balls to help England to victory.

An elegant batsman in all forms of the game, Sangakkara has scored 12,675 runs in One Day Internationals, more than any batsman currently playing. He has notched up 19 centuries and 85 fifties in one dayers with his highest score, 169, coming against South Africa in 2013. He was made ODI World Player of the Year in 2011 and 2013.

KUMAR SANGAKKARA

ICC Champions Trophy

Held every two years since 1998, the Champions Trophy is the second biggest ODI tournament after the ICC World Cup. At the 2013 tournament, England beat Australia, New Zealand and South Africa to reach the final, only to lose to India by five runs in a nailbiting match.

Ravi Bopara plays in the 2013 ICC Champions Trophy final. Despite scoring 30 and taking 3 for 20, Bopara finished on the losing side.

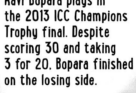

17

MOST ODI RUNS	
18,426	Sachin Tendulkar, India
13,704	Ricky Ponting, Australia
13,430	Sanath Jayasuriya, Sri Lanka
12,675	Kumar Sangakkara, Sri Lanka
11,739	Inzamam-ul-Haq, Pakistan

The ICC World Cup

The pinnacle of ODI action, the ICC World Cup is held once every four years. The first tournament, won by the West Indies, was held in England in 1975. Eagerly anticipated, the World Cup usually features a feast of attacking batting and bowling as sides contest 50-overs-per-side games, going all out for wins in the hope of reaching the final.

Super shocks

The World Cup throws up some sensational shock results as the smaller teams take a tilt at more established sides. At the 2003 World Cup, Kenya beat Sri Lanka and reached the semi-finals of the tournament. In 2011, England posted a large total – 327 runs – yet Ireland overcame it, courtesy of Kevin O'Brien's stunning innings of 113 off just 63 balls.

Kevin O'Brien sweeps the ball past Matt Prior during his match-winning innings in 2011.

The ICC World Cup trophy.

CRICKET WORLD CUP FINALS		
Year	Winners	Runners-up
2011	India	Sri Lanka
2007	Australia	Sri Lanka
2003	Australia	India
1999	Australia	Pakistan
1996	Sri Lanka	Australia
1992	Pakistan	England
1987	Australia	England
1983	India	West Indies
1979	West Indies	England
1975	West Indies	Australia

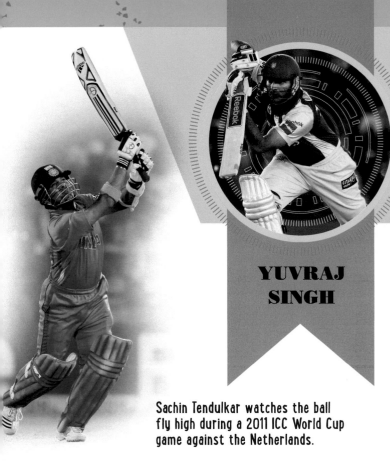

A clever one-day batsman and spin bowler, Singh had an epic 2011 World Cup for India. He won four Man of the Match awards during the tournament, scored 362 runs and took 15 wickets. His batting average was an astonishing 90.5 runs for each time he was out and he was duly awarded Player of the Tournament.

YUVRAJ SINGH

Sachin Tendulkar watches the ball fly high during a 2011 ICC World Cup game against the Netherlands.

2011 WORLD CUP STATS

Most sixes

36	New Zealand
34	West Indies

Most fours

235	India
226	Sri Lanka

Highest individual score

175	Virender Sehwag, India
158	Andrew Strauss, England

Most wickets

21	Shahid Afridi, Pakistan
21	Zaheer Khan, India

The 2015 World Cup

Hosted jointly by Australia and New Zealand, the 2015 competition features 49 games, with the final being held at the 100,000-capacity Melbourne Cricket Ground. The 14 teams taking part (including Ireland, Scotland and debutants, Afghanistan) are split into two groups of seven. They play each of the other six teams in their group in a league format. The top four teams in each group enter the quarter finals, just two matches away from the final.

Winners and losers

Australia are the only team to have won the tournament three times in a row, whilst England are the only team to make the final three times without ever becoming champions. India became the first side to win the competition as hosts (hosting jointly with Bangladesh and Sri Lanka) in 2011, at a tournament which attracted 1.2 million live spectators. Two legends of cricket hold key World Cup records. Glenn McGrath has taken the most wickets (72) whilst Sachin Tendulkar has scored the most runs (2,278).

Australia, led by Ricky Ponting (left), were knocked out at the quarter final stage of the 2011 competition.

The ICC Women's Cricket World Cup

The biggest tournament in women's cricket, the Women's World Cup was first held in 1973, and was won by England. Early tournaments were dominated by England, Australia and New Zealand but the World Cup is becoming more competitive. At the 2013 tournament, Sri Lanka defeated England and India whilst the West Indies beat New Zealand and Australia.

Arran Brindle comes into bowl during the third-fourth playoff game at the 2013 Women's World Cup. Brindle's two wickets helped England win the match.

Tournament milestones

The 1997 World Cup was the first to be played in a 50 rather than 60 overs-per-side format and was also the scene of the highest ever innings, when Australia's Belinda Davies struck 229 runs not out against Zimbabwe. The 2005 World Cup saw the closest ever finish when South Africa beat the West Indies by just one run, whilst the 2009 competition saw the most sixes hit – 47, including nine by New Zealand in one innings.

LEADING WICKET-TAKERS AT THE 2013 WOMEN'S WORLD CUP

15	Megan Schutt	Australia
13	Anya Shrubsole	England
12	Katherine Brun	England
12	Sian Ruck	New Zealand
11	Arran Brindle	England

HIGHEST TOTALS AT THE WOMEN'S WORLD CUP

412 for 3	Australia v Denmark	1997
376 for 2	England v Pakistan	1997
373 for 7	New Zealand v Pakistan	2009
368 for 8	West Indies v Sri Lanka	2013
324 for 3	England v Ireland	1997

Australia celebrate taking a wicket against the West Indies in the 2013 final.

Three of the four highest century makers at the Women's World Cup are English: Charlotte Edwards, Jan Brittin and Sarah Taylor. Australian legend Karen Rolton is the other. Brittin is also the competition's all-time leading catcher, with 19 catches made.

Suzie Bates plays an attacking shot. She has scored over 2,000 ODI runs including 682 at two World Cups.

SUZIE BATES

An aggressive, risk-taking batsman, Bates has scored over 2,000 runs in ODIs and has performed brilliantly at World Cups. At the 2009 tournament, her sensational innings of 168 from just 105 balls propelled New Zealand into the final. Four years later, she was the 2013 World Cup's leading scorer with 407 runs, and was named Women's ODI Cricketer of the Year. Bates also played basketball for New Zealand at the 2008 Olympics.

Recent tournaments

England triumphed at the 2009 World Cup, beating New Zealand in an exciting final. Claire Taylor scored 324 runs, more than anyone else, and was made Player of the Tournament. Four years later in a tournament hosted in India, Australia became champions for a record sixth time when they beat the West Indies by 114 runs in the final. A fine 106 not out by England captain, Charlotte Edwards, saw England beat New Zealand to come third.

First class cricket

First class cricket sees each team play two innings in matches that are usually held over four days. Each cricketing country has its own important first class competition, from the Plunkett Shield in New Zealand to the Regional Four Day Competition in the West Indies, which was won six out of seven times by Jamaica between 2008 and 2014.

In 2013, Essex were all out for just 20 runs to their County Championship rivals, Lancashire, who scored 398 in their innings! Amazingly, this isn't the lowest score made by a team in the County Championship. That honour goes to Northampton, who were bowled out for 12 back in 1907.

COUNTY CHAMPIONS SINCE 2000

2000 Surrey
2001 Yorkshire
2002 Surrey
2003 Sussex
2004 Warwickshire
2005 Nottinghamshire
2006 Sussex
2007 Sussex
2008 Durham
2009 Durham
2010 Nottinghamshire
2011 Lancashire
2012 Warwickshire
2013 Durham
2014 Yorkshire

The County Championship

The oldest first class cricket competition in the world began in England in 1880. The County Championship features 18 teams which, since 2000, play in two divisions. At the end of each season, two teams are promoted from the second division and two relegated from the first – which has added extra tension to games. Lancashire were champions in 2011 but were relegated the following year, only to bounce back and get promoted again in 2013.

Northamptonshire's Andrew Hall bats in a 2014 County Championship game versus Middlesex.

Brian Lara scored over 22,000 runs for the West Indies in Tests and ODIs and played for first class teams in four different countries (the West Indies, England, South Africa and Zimbabwe). Whilst playing for Warwickshire in the County Championship in 1994, Lara struck a remarkable 501 not out – the highest ever first class score. A whopping 308 of those runs were fours or sixes!

BRIAN LARA

Steve Smith holds the imposing Sheffield Shield trophy after leading New South Wales to glory in 2014.

The Sheffield Shield

Australia's leading first class competition is between the six states that make up the country: Queensland, Victoria, New South Wales, South Australia, Western Australia and Tasmania. Each side plays the others twice in a season with the top two sides playing a one-off game to determine the champions. New South Wales, led by Steve Smith, were the winners in 2014.

Fast bowler Steve Harmison roars in for the Highveld Lions in their SuperSport Series match versus the Nashua Cape Cobras.

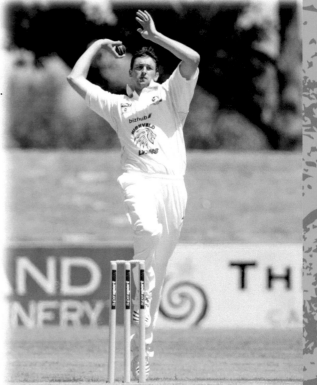

India and South Africa

South Africa's first class championship is known as the Sunfoil Series (formerly the SuperSport Series and before that the Currie Cup). It features six teams battling it out over 10 first class matches in a competition won in 2013 and 2014 by Cape Cobras. India's Ranji Trophy features 27 teams divided into three groups. The top four teams from Group A and Group B contest a knockout competition to decide the champions which, in 2014, were Karnataka.

Test match cricket

Test matches are five-day games between the world's best national cricket teams. Each side has two innings to score as many runs as possible whilst striving to bowl the other team out for fewer runs. For many talented young cricketers, representing their country in a Test match is the ultimate dream.

Tense tests

Australia beat England by 45 runs in the first Test match all the way back in 1877. Over 2,100 Tests have been played since then. Most are played in series lasting two to six matches. The balance in Test matches can change suddenly, with one team then the other gaining the advantage. Despite the long periods of play, pressure on players each ball can be incredibly intense. Test cricket is a test of a player's nerve as well as his or her skill.

In the past, Test matches were played until both teams completed their batting, which led to some long matches. In 1939, England and South Africa had to abandon their Test match as a draw after nine days as the England team had to catch their ship home!

FASTEST TEST HUNDREDS

Balls	Player	Match
56	Viv Richards	West Indies v England, 1986
57	Adam Gilchrist	Australia v England, 2006
67	Jack Gregory	Australia v South Africa, 1921
69	Shivnarine Chanderpaul	West Indies v Australia, 2003
69	David Warner	Australia v India, 2012

Sri Lanka set an attacking field with lots of fielders surrounding England's Jimmy Anderson.

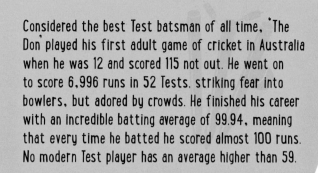

Considered the best Test batsman of all time, 'The Don' played his first adult game of cricket in Australia when he was 12 and scored 115 not out. He went on to score 6,996 runs in 52 Tests, striking fear into bowlers, but adored by crowds. He finished his career with an incredible batting average of 99.94, meaning that every time he batted he scored almost 100 runs. No modern Test player has an average higher than 59.

SIR DONALD BRADMAN

New ball and declarations

Play at Tests usually lasts 90 overs per day. Every 80 overs, the fielding team are offered a chance to replace the old, soft ball with a new ball, harder and with more bounce – perfect for their fast bowlers. Teams bat until they have lost all 10 of their wickets or, if they think they've enough runs, can declare (stop their innings and put the other team into bat). The highest ever Test score ended in a declaration as Sri Lanka scored 952 for 6 declared against India in 1997.

25

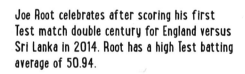

Joe Root celebrates after scoring his first Test match double century for England versus Sri Lanka in 2014. Root has a high Test batting average of 50.94.

Chris Jordan comes in to bowl during a 2014 Test match versus India. Jordan took seven wickets during the match.

NARROWEST WIN BY RUNS			
Margin	Winners	Opponents	Year
1 run	West Indies	Australia	1993
2 runs	England	Australia	2005
3 runs	Australia	England	1902
3 runs	England	Australia	1982

Test nations

Ten nations today play Test match cricket, with Bangladesh becoming the latest to join the party in 2000. Many of these sides have built up fierce rivalries over the years. So, when they come together to play a Test series, the excitement and anticipation can be huge, especially for series such as the Ashes (see p28-29), Pakistan versus India, or when Australia and India compete for the Border-Gavaskar Trophy.

Blistering bowling

Teams have to bowl the other side out twice to win a Test so they tend to select their most attacking bowlers to play. Aggressive bowlers like South African Dale Steyn, who took six Pakistan wickets for just eight runs in a 2013 Test, are expected to take wickets early on to put pressure on their opponents. Two bowlers have taken all 10 wickets in a Test innings (Jim Laker of England and India's Anil Kumble), but a top bowling performance by one player doesn't guarantee success. India's Javagal Srinath took 13 Pakistan wickets in a 1998 Test match but still finished on the losing side.

Stuart Broad appeals to the umpire during a 2014 Test match versus Sri Lanka.

TEST NATIONS				
Team	Matches	Wins	Draws	First Test
England	952	339	338	1877
Australia	767	360	202	1877
West Indies	500	163	168	1928
India	483	122	206	1932
New Zealand	394	77	158	1930
South Africa	387	142	116	1889
Pakistan	382	118	155	1952
Sri Lanka	233	71	80	1982
Zimbabwe	94	11	26	1992
Bangladesh	85	4	11	2000

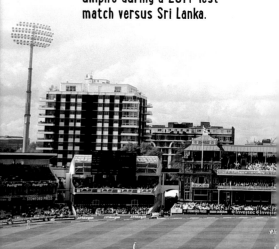

The England women's team pose for a photo after winning the Women's Ashes Test at the WACA ground in Perth, Australia in 2014.

In 2014, New Zealand's Mark Craig became the first player ever to hit their first ball in Test match cricket for a six. He ended up taking eight West Indies wickets and winning the Man of the Match award as well. Some debut!

Women's Tests

These games are similar to the men's matches, except they are played over four days rather than five, with more overs (100) bowled each day. They are not as commonly played as men's Tests but even so England's Jan Brittin has managed to amass a record 1,935 runs in Tests. Charlotte Edwards is not far behind on 1,621, 73 of which were scored in England's 2014 Test win over Australia.

MOST TEST MATCH RUNS

Player	Matches	Runs	Centuries
Sachin Tendulkar	200	15921	51
Ricky Ponting	168	13378	41
Jacques Kallis	166	13289	45
Rahul Dravid	164	13288	36
Brian Lara	131	11953	34

Saving the day

Sometimes, one team are in real trouble but dig in to save the game. In a 2014 Test against India, New Zealand were facing defeat until Brendan McCullum came in and struck 302 – the highest ever score by a New Zealander – to help draw the match. An even bigger turnaround occurred when Sri Lanka were 14 for 2 against South Africa in 2006. By the time South Africa next took a wicket, the score had raced up to 638 as Kumar Sangakkara and Mahela Jayawardene formed a world record partnership.

Considered the spiritual home of cricket, Lords cricket ground in London is packed with fans for the start of a Test match between England and New Zealand.

The Ashes

The most followed Test series in the world is also the oldest. The Ashes pits old foes England and Australia head to head for the prize of a tiny urn. This is believed to contain the ashes of the wooden bails from the wicket burned after an 1882 match between the two sides. In reality, the teams are playing for pride and honour – winning the Ashes is a big deal.

Sensational series

The Ashes normally occur every two years and are held over five matches (although in 1997, there were six matches in the series). The games are sell-outs at some of the most famous grounds in world cricket, including Lords in London and the massive MCG (Melbourne Cricket Ground) in Australia.

Two series in one year

In 2013 and 2014, to readjust world cricket schedules, two series were played in just six months. The first, in England, saw England win with Ian Bell scoring the most runs in the series (562) and Stuart Broad taking 11 wickets in one match. The return series, in Australia, saw fiery fast bowler Mitchell Johnson grab 37 wickets as Australia triumphed 5-0, only the third time one team has won all the matches in a series.

England captain Alistair Cook (right) holds the Ashes urn alongside teammates Ian Bell and Tim Bresnan after England won the 2013 series in England.

HIGHEST ASHES INNINGS BY CURRENT PLAYERS		
235 not out	Alistair Cook	Brisbane, 2010
227	Kevin Pietersen	Adelaide, 2010
195	Michael Hussey	Brisbane, 2010
189	Alistair Cook	Sydney, 2011
187	Michael Clarke	Manchester, 2013

England's Ben Stokes is out, caught, during the third Ashes Test of the 2013/14 series. Stokes ended the series as England's third highest run-scorer.

Australia's captain led them to Ashes glory in the 2013/14 series. A superb batsman, Clarke has scored 2,109 runs in Ashes Tests alone, including seven centuries, the highest of which was an innings of 187 scored in 2013 at Old Trafford in Manchester. He has also taken 29 catches in Ashes matches.

MICHAEL CLARKE

Mitchell Johnson claims one of his seven wickets during England's first innings in the 2013/14 second Ashes Test.

MOST ASHES WICKETS BY CURRENT PLAYERS

Wickets	Player	Best figures
77	Jimmy Anderson	5/73
72	Mitchell Johnson	7/40
67	Peter Siddle	6/54
63	Stuart Broad	6/50
57	Ryan Harris	7/117

To and fro

Both teams have enjoyed periods of success. From 1989 to 2005, Australia were dominant, with players like Shane Warne, Glenn McGrath and Steve Waugh helping them win the Ashes every time. Inspired by players like Andrew Flintoff and Kevin Pietersen, England won in 2005, and then won three of the next four series before Australia got their revenge in the 2013/14 series. This leaves the overall Ashes series poised at 32 series wins to Australia, 31 to England, and five series drawn.

Glossary

All-rounder A player capable of both bowling and batting well.

Appeal When a bowler or a bowler's teammate asks the umpire if the batsman is out and should lose his or her wicket.

Ashes A Test match series between England and Australia played roughly every two years.

Average (batting) The number of runs scored in a career or season divided by the number of innings in which the batsman was out.

Average (bowling) The number of runs scored off a bowler's overs divided by the number of wickets he has taken.

Bails The wooden rods placed on top of the stumps to form a wicket.

Boundary The edge of a cricket field and the name given to a batsman hitting the ball over it to score a four or six.

Century A score of 100 or more runs scored by an individual batsman.

Declaration When the batting side finishes their innings early before all of their players are out.

Delivery The word used to describe a ball bowled at the batsman by a bowler.

ICC Short for the International Cricket Council, the body that runs world cricket.

LBW Short for Leg Before Wicket, it is one of the ways a batsman can be out.

Leg side The area of the pitch behind the batsman's legs when he faces the ball.

ODIs Short for One Day Internationals which, today, are 50 overs-per-side matches played between national teams.

Off side The side of the pitch which is to a batsman's right (if right-handed), or left (if left-handed).

Over A series of six legal deliveries bowled by a bowler from one end of the pitch.

Partnership The number of runs scored by a pair of batsman.

Relegated To drop down a division of a cricket league for the following season.

Test match The ultimate form of cricket, a Test match is played over five days with two innings per side.

Twenty20 A form of the game where each side bats a maximum of 20 overs each.

Umpires The officials who control a cricket match and make key decisions on whether a player is out or not and whether runs have been scored.

Wide A ball which bounces so high or lands so wide of the stumps that it is very hard for a batsman to reach it.

Further information

Inside Sport: Cricket by Clive Gifford, Wayland, 2014.
A comprehensive look at the sport of cricket around the world.

Sporting Skills: Cricket by Clive Gifford, Wayland, 2014.
Learn how to perfect the skills, tactics and theory of cricket.

Great Sporting Events: Cricket by Clive Gifford, Franklin Watts, 2011.
A look at the top cricket competitions in the world, the history behind them and the players that have shaped them.

http://www.espncricinfo.com
A feature- and stat-packed website with profiles on all leading players and thousands of cricket records.

http://www.iplt20.com
The official website of the Indian Premier League. The site contains lots of news, features and profiles of teams and leading players.

http://www.bbc.co.uk/sport/0/cricket/womens
These BBC webpages cover women's cricket with fixtures, results and links to other sites.

http://www.icc-cricket.com/cricket-world-cup
The official website of the ICC Cricket World Cup 2015 with details of the grounds and teams involved.

http://www.cricket20.com
A great website for fans of Twenty20 cricket with news and features of all leading T20 tournaments.

http://www.ecb.co.uk/development/education/kwik-cricket
Check out the rules of Kwik Cricket and learn more about playing the game at this webpage.

http://www.cricket.com.au/get-involved/play-cricket/kids-cricket
Get involved in playing and watching live cricket at this website organised by Cricket Australia.

Index

Afghanistan 5, 9, 16
Afridi, Shahid 5, 19
Ashes, the 26, 28-29, 30
Australia 4, 6, 7, 8, 9, 12, 13, 14, 16, 17, 18, 19, 20, 21, 23, 24, 25, 26, 27, 28, 29

Bangladesh 13, 26
Bates, Suzie 21
batsmen and batting 4, 5, 6, 7, 8, 9, 11, 12, 14, 15, 16, 17, 18, 19, 21, 24, 25, 27, 29
beach cricket 6
Bell, Ian 5, 28
Big Bash 8, 9
boundaries 8, 11, 15, 30
bowlers & bowling 4, 7, 8, 9, 13, 14, 16, 18, 20, 22, 24, 25, 26, 27
  fast 11, 25, 28
  spin 19
Bradman, Sir Donald 25
Brittin, Jan 21, 27
Broad, Stuart 26, 28, 29

Caribbean Premier League 8, 9
Clarke, Michael 28, 29
Cook, Alistair 28
Craig, Mark 27
crowds 4, 8, 10, 25

Edwards, Charlotte 7, 21, 27
England 4, 5, 6, 8, 9, 12, 13, 14, 16, 17, 18, 19, 20, 21, 22, 23, 24, 25, 26, 27, 28, 29

fielders & fielding 4, 6, 7, 8, 13, 15, 24
Finch, Aaron 8, 9
first class cricket 22-23

Gayle, Chris 11
Gul, Umar 13

ICC Champions Trophy 17
ICC Women's Cricket World Cup 20-21
ICC World Cup 17, 18-19
ICC World Twenty20 12-13
India 4, 5, 9, 10-11, 13, 17, 18, 19, 20, 21, 23, 24, 25, 26, 27
Indian Premier League (IPL) 10-11
indoor cricket 6
innings 11, 14, 16, 18, 20, 21, 22, 24, 25, 26, 28, 29
International Cricket Council (ICC) 5
Ireland 6, 9, 18, 20

Jayawardene, Mahela 12, 27
Johnson, Mitchell 28, 29

Kenya 9, 18
Kohli, Virat 13
Kwik Cricket 7

Lara, Brian 23, 27
limited overs cricket 14-15, 16
Lords 17, 27, 28

Malaysia 9
Malinga, Lasith 11
McCullum, Brendan 27
Mendis, Ajantha 13

New Zealand 9, 13, 15, 17, 19, 20, 21, 22, 26, 27

O'Brien, Kevin 18
One Day Internationals (ODIs) 5, 7, 13, 16-17, 18-19, 23, 30
overs 8, 14, 15, 16, 18, 20, 25, 27, 30

Pakistan 4, 5, 6, 12, 13, 17, 18, 20, 26

Pietersen, Kevin 12, 28, 29
Ponting, Ricky 17, 19, 27
power plays 15

runs 5, 6, 7, 8, 9, 11, 12, 13, 14, 15, 16, 17, 18, 19, 20, 21, 22, 23, 24, 25, 26, 27, 28, 29
  centuries 5, 7, 8, 13, 17, 21, 29, 30
  fours 9, 11, 19, 23
  sixes 9, 11, 19, 20, 23, 27

Sangakkara, Kumar 17, 27
Shah, Saijida 6
Singh, Yuvraj 12, 19
South Africa 5, 6, 9, 12, 13, 14, 16, 17, 20, 23, 24, 26, 27
Sri Lanka 6, 9, 11, 12, 13, 14, 16, 17, 18, 19, 20, 24, 25, 26, 27
street cricket 6
Styris, Scott 8
Suppiah, Arul 9

Taylor, Claire 21
Taylor, Sarah 7, 21
Tendulkar, Sachin 17, 19, 27
Test matches 4, 5, 7, 16, 23, 24-25, 26-27, 28-29, 30
Twenty20 (T20) 5, 7, 8-9, 10-11, 12-13, 14, 30

Vaas, Chaminda 16

West Indies 4, 9, 11, 13, 14, 18, 19, 20, 21, 22, 23, 24, 25, 26, 27
wicketkeepers 7, 13
wickets 28
  taking 6, 9, 11, 13, 16, 19, 20, 21, 25, 26, 27, 28, 29
women's cricket 6, 7, 9, 13, 20-21, 27
world records 9, 13, 16, 27

Zimbabwe 5, 13, 16, 20, 23, 26